HAL•LEONARD

JAZZ PLAY ALONG®

Book and CD for B♭, E♭ and C Instruments

Volume 54

Arranged and Produced
by Mark Taylor

Moonlight in Vermont

AND OTHER GREAT STANDARDS

10 Jazz Classics

BOOK

TITLE	C Treble Instruments	B♭ Instruments	E♭ Instruments	C Bass Instruments
	PAGE NUMBERS			
A Child Is Born	4	20	36	52
Just Squeeze Me (But Don't Tease Me)	6	22	38	54
Love You Madly	8	24	40	56
Lover Man (Oh, Where Can You Be?)	5	21	37	53
Moonlight in Vermont	10	26	42	58
My Old Flame	12	28	44	60
The Night Has a Thousand Eyes	14	30	46	62
Small Fry	13	29	45	61
A Sunday Kind of Love	16	32	48	64
You Brought a New Kind of Love to Me	18	34	50	66

CD

TITLE	CD Track Number Split Track / Melody	CD Track Number Full Stereo Track
A Child Is Born	1	2
Just Squeeze Me (But Don't Tease Me)	3	4
Love You Madly	5	6
Lover Man (Oh, Where Can You Be?)	7	8
Moonlight in Vermont	9	10
My Old Flame	11	12
The Night Has a Thousand Eyes	13	14
Small Fry	15	16
A Sunday Kind of Love	17	18
You Brought a New Kind of Love to Me	19	20
B♭ Tuning Notes		21

ISBN 0-634-09083-6

HAL•LEONARD® CORPORATION

7777 W. BLUEMOUND RD. P.O. BOX 13819 MILWAUKEE, WI 53213

For all works contained herein:
Unauthorized copying, arranging, adapting, recording or public performance is an infringement of copyright.
Infringers are liable under the law.

Visit Hal Leonard Online at
www.halleonard.com

Moonlight in Vermont & Other Great Standards

HAL•LEONARD
JAZZ PLAY ALONG®

Volume 54

Arranged and Produced by
Mark Taylor

Featured Players:

Graham Breedlove–Trumpet
John Desalme–Saxophones
Tony Nalker–Piano
Jim Roberts–Bass
Steve Fidyk–Drums

Recorded at Bias Studios, Springfield, Virginia
Bob Dawson, Engineer

HOW TO USE THE CD:

Each song has <u>two</u> tracks:

1) Split Track/Melody

Woodwind, Brass, Keyboard, and Mallet Players can use this track as a learning tool for melody style and inflection.

Bass Players can learn and perform with this track – remove the recorded bass track by turning down the volume on the LEFT channel.

Keyboard and **Guitar Players** can learn and perform with this track – remove the recorded piano part by turning down the volume on the RIGHT channel.

2) Full Stereo Track

Soloists or **Groups** can learn and perform with this accompaniment track with the RHYTHM SECTION only.

A CHILD IS BORN

BY THAD JONES

Copyright © 1969 D'Accord Music, Inc., c/o Publishers' Licensing Corporation, P.O. Box 5807, Englewood, New Jersey 07631
Copyright Renewed
This arrangement Copyright © 2006 D'Accord Music, Inc., c/o Publishers' Licensing Corporation, P.O. Box 5807, Englewood, New Jersey 07631
All Rights Reserved

LOVER MAN
(OH, WHERE CAN YOU BE?)

BY JIMMY DAVIS, ROGER RAMIREZ
AND JIMMY SHERMAN

Copyright © 1941, 1942 UNIVERSAL MUSIC CORP.
Copyright Renewed
This arrangement Copyright © 2006 UNIVERSAL MUSIC CORP.
All Rights Reserved   Used by Permission

JUST SQUEEZE ME
(BUT DON'T TEASE ME)

WORDS BY LEE GAINES
MUSIC BY DUKE ELLINGTON

C VERSION

Copyright © 1946 (Renewed 1974) by Famous Music Corporation and EMI Robbins Catalog Inc. in the U.S.A.
This arrangement Copyright © 2006 by Famous Music Corporation and EMI Robbins Catalog Inc. in the U.S.A.
Rights for the world outside the U.S.A. Controlled by EMI Robbins Catalog Inc. and Warner Bros. Publications U.S. Inc.
International Copyright Secured   All Rights Reserved

LOVE YOU MADLY

BY DUKE ELLINGTON

Copyright © 1950 (Renewed 1977) and Assigned to Famous Music Corporation in the U.S.A.
This arrangement Copyright © 2006 by Famous Music Corporation in the U.S.A.
Rights for the world outside the U.S.A. Controlled by Tempo Music, Inc. c/o Music Sales Corporation and Famous Music Corporation
International Copyright Secured   All Rights Reserved

MOONLIGHT IN VERMONT

WORDS AND MUSIC BY JOHN BLACKBURN
AND KARL SUESSDORF

C VERSION

Copyright © 1944 (Renewed 1972) Michael H. Goldsen, Inc.
Copyright Renewed 2000 Michael H. Goldsen, Inc. and Johnny R. Music Company in the U.S.
This arrangement Copyright © 2006 Michael H. Goldsen, Inc. and Johnny R. Music Company in the U.S.
All Rights outside the U.S. Controlled by Michael H. Goldsen, Inc.
International Copyright Secured   All Rights Reserved

MY OLD FLAME

CD
11 : SPLIT TRACK/MELODY
12 : FULL STEREO TRACK

WORDS AND MUSIC BY ARTHUR JOHNSTON
AND SAM COSLOW

C VERSION

Copyright © 1934 (Renewed 1961) by Famous Music Corporation
This arrangement Copyright © 2006 by Famous Music Corporation
International Copyright Secured All Rights Reserved

SMALL FRY

WORDS BY FRANK LOESSER
MUSIC BY HOAGY CARMICHAEL

CD
15 : SPLIT TRACK/MELODY
16 : FULL STEREO TRACK

C VERSION

Copyright © 1938 (Renewed 1965) by Famous Music Corporation
This arrangement Copyright © 2006 by Famous Music Corporation
International Copyright Secured   All Rights Reserved

CD

13: SPLIT TRACK/MELODY
14: FULL STEREO TRACK

THE NIGHT HAS A THOUSAND EYES

WORDS BY BUDDY BERNIER
MUSIC BY JERRY BRAININ

C VERSION

Copyright © 1948 (Renewed 1975) by Paramount Music Corporation
This arrangement Copyright © 2006 by Paramount Music Corporation
International Copyright Secured   All Rights Reserved

A Sunday Kind of Love

CD
🎵17: SPLIT TRACK/MELODY
🎵18: FULL STEREO TRACK

WORDS AND MUSIC BY BARBARA BELLE,
LOUIS PRIMA, ANITA LEONARD AND STAN RHODES

C VERSION   MED. SWING

Copyright © 1946 UNIVERSAL MUSIC
All Rights Assigned to UNIVERSAL MUSIC CORP. and LGL MUSIC in the extended term
Copyright Renewed
This arrangement Copyright © 2006 UNIVERSAL MUSIC CORP. and LGL MUSIC
All Rights Reserved   Used by Permission

CD

◆19◆: SPLIT TRACK/MELODY

◆20◆: FULL STEREO TRACK

C VERSION

YOU BROUGHT A NEW KIND OF LOVE TO ME

WORDS AND MUSIC BY SAMMY FAIN,
IRVING KAHAL AND PIERRE NORMAN

Copyright © 1930 (Renewed 1957) by Famous Music Corporation
This arrangement Copyright © 2006 by Famous Music Corporation
International Copyright Secured   All Rights Reserved

A CHILD IS BORN

BY THAD JONES

Copyright © 1969 D'Accord Music, Inc., c/o Publishers' Licensing Corporation, P.O. Box 5807, Englewood, New Jersey 07631
Copyright Renewed
This arrangement Copyright © 2006 D'Accord Music, Inc., c/o Publishers' Licensing Corporation, P.O. Box 5807, Englewood, New Jersey 07631
All Rights Reserved

LOVER MAN
(OH, WHERE CAN YOU BE?)

BY JIMMY DAVIS, ROGER RAMIREZ
AND JIMMY SHERMAN

CD
7 : SPLIT TRACK/MELODY
8 : FULL STEREO TRACK

MOLTO RIT.

Copyright © 1941, 1942 UNIVERSAL MUSIC CORP.
Copyright Renewed
This arrangement Copyright © 2006 UNIVERSAL MUSIC CORP.
All Rights Reserved   Used by Permission

JUST SQUEEZE ME
(BUT DON'T TEASE ME)

WORDS BY LEE GAINES
MUSIC BY DUKE ELLINGTON

Copyright © 1946 (Renewed 1974) by Famous Music Corporation and EMI Robbins Catalog Inc. in the U.S.A.
This arrangement Copyright © 2006 by Famous Music Corporation and EMI Robbins Catalog Inc. in the U.S.A.
Rights for the world outside the U.S.A. Controlled by EMI Robbins Catalog Inc. and Warner Bros. Publications U.S. Inc.
International Copyright Secured   All Rights Reserved

Love You Madly

BY Duke Ellington

Copyright © 1950 (Renewed 1977) and Assigned to Famous Music Corporation in the U.S.A.
This arrangement Copyright © 2006 by Famous Music Corporation in the U.S.A.
Rights for the world outside the U.S.A. Controlled by Tempo Music, Inc. c/o Music Sales Corporation and Famous Music Corporation
International Copyright Secured   All Rights Reserved

PIANO

Moonlight in Vermont

WORDS AND MUSIC BY JOHN BLACKBURN
AND KARL SUESSDORF

CD
: SPLIT TRACK/MELODY
: FULL STEREO TRACK

B♭ VERSION

JAZZ WALTZ

TO CODA ⊕

Copyright © 1944 (Renewed 1972) Michael H. Goldsen, Inc.
Copyright Renewed 2000 Michael H. Goldsen, Inc. and Johnny R. Music Company in the U.S.
This arrangement Copyright © 2006 Michael H. Goldsen, Inc. and Johnny R. Music Company in the U.S.
All Rights outside the U.S. Controlled by Michael H. Goldsen, Inc.
International Copyright Secured   All Rights Reserved

MY OLD FLAME

WORDS AND MUSIC BY ARTHUR JOHNSTON
AND SAM COSLOW

Copyright © 1934 (Renewed 1961) by Famous Music Corporation
This arrangement Copyright © 2006 by Famous Music Corporation
International Copyright Secured   All Rights Reserved

SMALL FRY

WORDS BY FRANK LOESSER
MUSIC BY HOAGY CARMICHAEL

CD
15 : SPLIT TRACK/MELODY
16 : FULL STEREO TRACK

Bb VERSION   BOSSA

Copyright © 1938 (Renewed 1965) by Famous Music Corporation
This arrangement Copyright © 2006 by Famous Music Corporation
International Copyright Secured   All Rights Reserved

The Night Has a Thousand Eyes

WORDS BY BUDDY BERNIER
MUSIC BY JERRY BRAININ

Copyright © 1948 (Renewed 1975) by Paramount Music Corporation
This arrangement Copyright © 2006 by Paramount Music Corporation
International Copyright Secured   All Rights Reserved

A Sunday Kind of Love

CD

▼17 : SPLIT TRACK/MELODY

▼18 : FULL STEREO TRACK

WORDS AND MUSIC BY BARBARA BELLE,
LOUIS PRIMA, ANITA LEONARD AND STAN RHODES

Bb VERSION

Copyright © 1946 UNIVERSAL MUSIC
All Rights Assigned to UNIVERSAL MUSIC CORP. and LGL MUSIC in the extended term
Copyright Renewed
This arrangement Copyright © 2006 UNIVERSAL MUSIC CORP. and LGL MUSIC
All Rights Reserved   Used by Permission

YOU BROUGHT A NEW KIND OF LOVE TO ME

WORDS AND MUSIC BY SAMMY FAIN,
IRVING KAHAL AND PIERRE NORMAN

Bb VERSION

Copyright © 1930 (Renewed 1957) by Famous Music Corporation
This arrangement Copyright © 2006 by Famous Music Corporation
International Copyright Secured   All Rights Reserved

A CHILD IS BORN

BY THAD JONES

Copyright © 1969 D'Accord Music, Inc., c/o Publishers' Licensing Corporation, P.O. Box 5807, Englewood, New Jersey 07631
Copyright Renewed
This arrangement Copyright © 2006 D'Accord Music, Inc., c/o Publishers' Licensing Corporation, P.O. Box 5807, Englewood, New Jersey 07631
All Rights Reserved

LOVER MAN
(OH, WHERE CAN YOU BE?)

BY JIMMY DAVIS, ROGER RAMIREZ
AND JIMMY SHERMAN

MOLTO RIT.

Copyright © 1941, 1942 UNIVERSAL MUSIC CORP.
Copyright Renewed
This arrangement Copyright © 2006 UNIVERSAL MUSIC CORP.
All Rights Reserved   Used by Permission

JUST SQUEEZE ME
(BUT DON'T TEASE ME)

WORDS BY LEE GAINES
MUSIC BY DUKE ELLINGTON

Copyright © 1946 (Renewed 1974) by Famous Music Corporation and EMI Robbins Catalog Inc. in the U.S.A.
This arrangement Copyright © 2006 by Famous Music Corporation and EMI Robbins Catalog Inc. in the U.S.A.
Rights for the world outside the U.S.A. Controlled by EMI Robbins Catalog Inc. and Warner Bros. Publications U.S. Inc.
International Copyright Secured   All Rights Reserved

LOVE YOU MADLY

BY DUKE ELLINGTON

Copyright © 1950 (Renewed 1977) and Assigned to Famous Music Corporation in the U.S.A.
This arrangement Copyright © 2006 by Famous Music Corporation in the U.S.A.
Rights for the world outside the U.S.A. Controlled by Tempo Music, Inc. c/o Music Sales Corporation and Famous Music Corporation
International Copyright Secured   All Rights Reserved

MOONLIGHT IN VERMONT

WORDS AND MUSIC BY JOHN BLACKBURN
AND KARL SUESSDORF

E♭ VERSION

CD
◆9◆ : SPLIT TRACK/MELODY
◆10◆ : FULL STEREO TRACK

Copyright © 1944 (Renewed 1972) Michael H. Goldsen, Inc.
Copyright Renewed 2000 Michael H. Goldsen, Inc. and Johnny R. Music Company in the U.S.
This arrangement Copyright © 2006 Michael H. Goldsen, Inc. and Johnny R. Music Company in the U.S.
All Rights outside the U.S. Controlled by Michael H. Goldsen, Inc.
International Copyright Secured All Rights Reserved

MY OLD FLAME

Copyright © 1934 (Renewed 1961) by Famous Music Corporation
This arrangement Copyright © 2006 by Famous Music Corporation
International Copyright Secured   All Rights Reserved

SMALL FRY

WORDS BY FRANK LOESSER
MUSIC BY HOAGY CARMICHAEL

Copyright © 1938 (Renewed 1965) by Famous Music Corporation
This arrangement Copyright © 2006 by Famous Music Corporation
International Copyright Secured   All Rights Reserved

THE NIGHT HAS A THOUSAND EYES

CD
13 : SPLIT TRACK/MELODY
14 : FULL STEREO TRACK

WORDS BY BUDDY BERNIER
MUSIC BY JERRY BRAININ

E♭ VERSION

Copyright © 1948 (Renewed 1975) by Paramount Music Corporation
This arrangement Copyright © 2006 by Paramount Music Corporation
International Copyright Secured   All Rights Reserved

A SUNDAY KIND OF LOVE

WORDS AND MUSIC BY BARBARA BELLE,
LOUIS PRIMA, ANITA LEONARD AND STAN RHODES

CD
17 : SPLIT TRACK/MELODY
18 : FULL STEREO TRACK

E♭ VERSION

Copyright © 1946 UNIVERSAL MUSIC
All Rights Assigned to UNIVERSAL MUSIC CORP. and LGL MUSIC in the extended term
Copyright Renewed
This arrangement Copyright © 2006 UNIVERSAL MUSIC CORP. and LGL MUSIC
All Rights Reserved   Used by Permission

YOU BROUGHT A NEW KIND OF LOVE TO ME

WORDS AND MUSIC BY SAMMY FAIN,
IRVING KAHAL AND PIERRE NORMAN

Eb VERSION

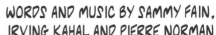

Copyright © 1930 (Renewed 1957) by Famous Music Corporation
This arrangement Copyright © 2006 by Famous Music Corporation
International Copyright Secured   All Rights Reserved

A CHILD IS BORN

BY THAD JONES

Copyright © 1969 D'Accord Music, Inc., c/o Publishers' Licensing Corporation, P.O. Box 5807, Englewood, New Jersey 07631
Copyright Renewed
This arrangement Copyright © 2006 D'Accord Music, Inc., c/o Publishers' Licensing Corporation, P.O. Box 5807, Englewood, New Jersey 07631
All Rights Reserved

LOVER MAN
(OH, WHERE CAN YOU BE?)

BY JIMMY DAVIS, ROGER RAMIREZ
AND JIMMY SHERMAN

Copyright © 1941, 1942 UNIVERSAL MUSIC CORP.
Copyright Renewed
This arrangement Copyright © 2006 UNIVERSAL MUSIC CORP.
All Rights Reserved   Used by Permission

Just Squeeze Me
(But Don't Tease Me)

WORDS BY LEE GAINES
MUSIC BY DUKE ELLINGTON

Copyright © 1946 (Renewed 1974) by Famous Music Corporation and EMI Robbins Catalog Inc. in the U.S.A.
This arrangement Copyright © 2006 by Famous Music Corporation and EMI Robbins Catalog Inc. in the U.S.A.
Rights for the world outside the U.S.A. Controlled by EMI Robbins Catalog Inc. and Warner Bros. Publications U.S. Inc.
International Copyright Secured   All Rights Reserved

Love You Madly

BY Duke Ellington

CD
◆5 : SPLIT TRACK/MELODY
◆6 : FULL STEREO TRACK

Copyright © 1950 (Renewed 1977) and Assigned to Famous Music Corporation in the U.S.A.
This arrangement Copyright © 2006 by Famous Music Corporation in the U.S.A.
Rights for the world outside the U.S.A. Controlled by Tempo Music, Inc. c/o Music Sales Corporation and Famous Music Corporation
International Copyright Secured   All Rights Reserved

SOLOS (2 CHORUSES)

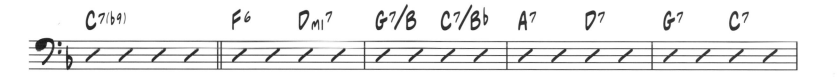

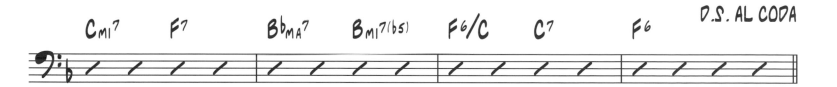

D.S. AL CODA

CODA

PIANO

MOONLIGHT IN VERMONT

WORDS AND MUSIC BY JOHN BLACKBURN
AND KARL SUESSDORF

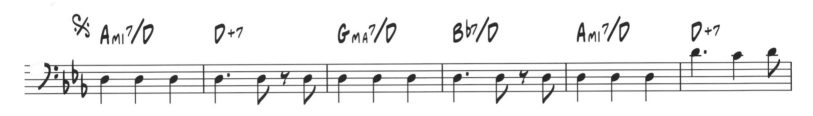

Copyright © 1944 (Renewed 1972) Michael H. Goldsen, Inc.
Copyright Renewed 2000 Michael H. Goldsen, Inc. and Johnny R. Music Company in the U.S.
This arrangement Copyright © 2006 Michael H. Goldsen, Inc. and Johnny R. Music Company in the U.S.
All Rights outside the U.S. Controlled by Michael H. Goldsen, Inc.
International Copyright Secured   All Rights Reserved

MY OLD FLAME

WORDS AND MUSIC BY ARTHUR JOHNSTON
AND SAM COSLOW

Copyright © 1934 (Renewed 1961) by Famous Music Corporation
This arrangement Copyright © 2006 by Famous Music Corporation
International Copyright Secured   All Rights Reserved

SMALL FRY

WORDS BY FRANK LOESSER
MUSIC BY HOAGY CARMICHAEL

Copyright © 1938 (Renewed 1965) by Famous Music Corporation
This arrangement Copyright © 2005 by Famous Music Corporation
International Copyright Secured   All Rights Reserved

THE NIGHT HAS A THOUSAND EYES

WORDS BY BUDDY BERNIER
MUSIC BY JERRY BRAININ

Copyright © 1948 (Renewed 1975) by Paramount Music Corporation
This arrangement Copyright © 2006 by Paramount Music Corporation
International Copyright Secured   All Rights Reserved

A SUNDAY KIND OF LOVE

WORDS AND MUSIC BY BARBARA BELLE,
LOUIS PRIMA, ANITA LEONARD AND STAN RHODES

Copyright © 1946 UNIVERSAL MUSIC
All Rights Assigned to UNIVERSAL MUSIC CORP. and LGL MUSIC in the extended term
Copyright Renewed
This arrangement Copyright © 2006 UNIVERSAL MUSIC CORP. and LGL MUSIC
All Rights Reserved   Used by Permission

YOU BROUGHT A NEW KIND OF LOVE TO ME

CD
19 : SPLIT TRACK/MELODY
20 : FULL STEREO TRACK

𝄢: C VERSION

WORDS AND MUSIC BY SAMMY FAIN,
IRVING KAHAL AND PIERRE NORMAN

Copyright © 1930 (Renewed 1957) by Famous Music Corporation
This arrangement Copyright © 2006 by Famous Music Corporation
International Copyright Secured   All Rights Reserved

 **Presenting the Hal Leonard** JAZZ PLAY ALONG SERIES

DUKE ELLINGTON Vol. 1 00841644
Caravan • Don't Get Around Much Anymore • In a Sentimental Mood • Perdido • Prelude to a Kiss • Satin Doll • Take the "A" Train • and more.

MILES DAVIS Vol. 2 00841645
All Blues • Blue in Green • Four • Half Nelson • Milestones • Nardis • Seven Steps to Heaven • So What • Solar • Tune Up.

THE BLUES Vol. 3 00841646
Billie's Bounce • Birk's Works • C-Jam Blues • Freddie Freeloader • Mr. P.C. • Tenor Madness • Things Ain't What They Used to Be • and more.

JAZZ BALLADS Vol. 4 00841691
Body and Soul • Here's That Rainy Day • Misty • My Funny Valentine • The Nearness of You • Polka Dots and Moonbeams • and more.

BEST OF BEBOP Vol. 5 00841689
Anthropology • Donna Lee • Doxy • Epistrophy • Lady Bird • Oleo • Ornithology • Scrapple from the Apple • Woodyn' You • Yardbird Suite.

JAZZ CLASSICS WITH EASY CHANGES Vol. 6 00841690
Blue Train • Comin' Home Baby • Footprints • Impressions • Killer Joe • St. Thomas • Well You Needn't • and more.

ESSENTIAL JAZZ STANDARDS Vol. 7 00843000
Autumn Leaves • Lullaby of Birdland • Stella by Starlight • There Will Never Be Another You • When Sunny Gets Blue • and more.

ANTONIO CARLOS JOBIM AND THE ART OF THE BOSSA NOVA Vol. 8 00843001
The Girl from Ipanema • How Insensitive • Meditation • One Note Samba • Quiet Nights of Quiet Stars • Slightly Out of Tune • and more.

DIZZY GILLESPIE Vol. 9 00843002
Birk's Works • Con Alma • Groovin' High • Manteca • A Night in Tunisia • Salt Peanuts • Tour De Force • Woodyn' You • and more.

DISNEY CLASSICS Vol. 10 00843003
Alice in Wonderland • Cruella De Vil • When You Wish upon a Star • You've Got a Friend in Me • Zip-a-Dee-Doo-Dah • and more.

RODGERS AND HART FAVORITES Vol. 11 00843004
Bewitched • Dancing on the Ceiling • Have You Met Miss Jones? • I Could Write a Book • The Lady Is a Tramp • My Romance • and more.

ESSENTIAL JAZZ CLASSICS Vol. 12 00843005
Airegin • Ceora • The Frim Fram Sauce • Israel • Milestones • Nefertiti • Red Clay • Satin Doll • Song for My Father • Take Five.

JOHN COLTRANE Vol. 13 00843006
Blue Train • Countdown • Cousin Mary • Equinox • Giant Steps • Impressions • Lazy Bird • Mr. P.C. • Moment's Notice • Naima.

IRVING BERLIN Vol. 14 00843007
Blue Skies • How Deep Is the Ocean • I've Got My Love to Keep Me Warm • Steppin' Out with My Baby • What'll I Do? • and more.

RODGERS & HAMMERSTEIN Vol. 15 00843008
Do I Love You Because You're Beautiful? • It Might as Well Be Spring • My Favorite Things • Younger Than Springtime • and more.

COLE PORTER Vol. 16 00843009
Easy to Love • I Concentrate on You • I've Got You Under My Skin • It's All Right with Me • It's De-Lovely • You'd Be So Nice to Come Home To • and more.

COUNT BASIE Vol. 17 00843010
All of Me • April in Paris • Blues in Hoss Flat • Li'l Darlin' • Moten Swing • One O'Clock Jump • Shiny Stockings • Until I Met You • and more.

HAROLD ARLEN Vol. 18 00843011
Ac-cent-tchu-ate the Positive • Come Rain or Come Shine • I've Got the World on a String • Stormy Weather • That Old Black Magic • and more.

COOL JAZZ Vol. 19 00843012
Bernie's Tune • Boplicity • Budo • Conception • Django • Five Brothers • Line for Lyons • Walkin' Shoes • Waltz for Debby • Whisper Not.

RODGERS AND HART CLASSICS Vol. 21 00843014
Falling in Love with Love • Isn't it Romantic? • Manhattan • My Funny Valentine • This Can't Be Love • Thou Swell • Where or When • and more.

WAYNE SHORTER Vol. 22 00843015
Children of the Night • ESP • Footprints • Juju • Mahjong • Nefertiti • Nightdreamer • Speak No Evil • Witch Hunt • Yes and No.

LATIN JAZZ Vol. 23 00843016
Agua De Beber • Chega De Saudade • Manha De Carnaval • Mas Que Nada • Ran Kan Kan • So Nice • Watch What Happens • and more.

EARLY JAZZ STANDARDS Vol. 24 00843017
After You've Gone • Avalon • Indian Summer • Indiana • Ja-Da • Limehouse Blues • Paper Doll • Poor Butterfly • Rose Room • St. Louis Blues.

CHRISTMAS JAZZ Vol. 25 00843018
The Christmas Song (Chestnuts Roasting on an Open Fire) • I'll Be Home for Christmas • Let It Snow! Let It Snow! Let It Snow! • Silver Bells • and more.

CHARLIE PARKER Vol. 26 00843019
Au Privave • Billie's Bounce • Donna Lee • My Little Suede Shoes • Ornithology • Scrapple from the Apple • Yardbird Suite • and more.

GREAT JAZZ STANDARDS Vol. 27 00843020
Fly Me to the Moon • How High the Moon • I Can't Get Started with You • Speak Low • Tangerine • Willow Weep for Me • and more.

BIG BAND ERA Vol. 28 00843021
Air Mail Special • Christopher Columbus • In the Mood • Jersey Bounce • Opus One • Stompin' at the Savoy • Tuxedo Junction • and more.

LENNON AND MCCARTNEY Vol. 29 00843022
And I Love Her • Blackbird • Come Together • Eleanor Rigby • Let It Be • Ticket to Ride • Yesterday • and more.

BLUES' BEST Vol. 30 00843023
Basin Street Blues • Bloomdido • Happy Go Lucky Local • K.C. Blues • Sonnymoon for Two • Take the Coltrane • Turnaround • Twisted • and more.

JAZZ IN THREE Vol. 31 00843024
Bluesette • Jitterbug Waltz • Moon River • Tennessee Waltz • West Coast Blues • What the World Needs Now Is Love • Wives and Lovers • and more.

BEST OF SWING Vol. 32 00843025
Alright, Okay, You Win • Cherokee • I'll Be Seeing You • Jump, Jive An' Wail • On the Sunny Side of the Street • Route 66 • Sentimental Journey • and more.

SONNY ROLLINS Vol. 33 00843029
Airegin • Alfie's Theme • Biji • The Bridge • Doxy • First Moves • Here's to the People • Oleo • St. Thomas • Sonnymoon for Two.

ALL TIME STANDARDS Vol. 34 00843030
Autumn in New York • Bye Bye Blackbird • Call Me Irresponsible • Georgia on My Mind • Honeysuckle Rose • Stardust • The Very Thought of You • more.

BLUESY JAZZ Vol. 35 00843031
Angel Eyes • Bags' Groove • Bessie's Blues • Chitlins Con Carne • Mercy, Mercy, Mercy • Night Train • Sweet Georgia Bright • and more.

HORACE SILVER Vol. 36 00843032
Doodlin' • The Jody Grind • Nica's Dream • Opus De Funk • Peace • The Preacher • Senor Blues • Sister Sadie • Song for My Father • Strollin'.

BILL EVANS Vol. 37 00843033 ($16.95)
Funkallero • My Bells • One for Helen • The Opener • Orbit • Show-Type Tune • 34 Skidoo • Time Remembered • Turn Out the Stars • Waltz for Debby.

YULETIDE JAZZ Vol. 38 00843034
Blue Christmas • Christmas Time Is Here • Merry Christmas, Darling • The Most Wonderful Time of the Year • Santa Claus Is Comin' to Town • and more.

"ALL THE THINGS YOU ARE" & MORE JEROME KERN SONGS Vol. 39 00843035
All the Things You Are • Can't Help Lovin' Dat Man • A Fine Romance • Long Ago (And Far Away) • The Way You Look Tonight • Yesterdays • and more.

BOSSA NOVA Vol. 40 00843036
Black Orpheus • Call Me • A Man and a Woman • Only Trust Your Heart • The Shadow of Your Smile • Watch What Happens • Wave • and more.

CLASSIC DUKE ELLINGTON Vol. 41 00843037
Cotton Tail • Do Nothin' Till You Hear from Me • I Got It Bad and That Ain't Good • I'm Beginning to See the Light • Mood Indigo • Solitude • and more.

GERRY MULLIGAN CLASSICS Vol. 43 00843039
Apple Core • Line for Lyons • Nights at the Turntable • Song for Strayhorn • Walkin' Shoes • and more.

OLIVER NELSON Vol. 44 00843040
The Drive • Emancipation Blues • Hoe-Down • I Remember Bird • Miss Fine • Stolen Moments • Straight Ahead • Teenie's Blues • Yearnin'.

JAZZ AT THE MOVIES Vol. 45 00843041
Baby Elephant Walk • God Bless' the Child • The Look of Love • The Rainbow Connection • Swinging on a Star • Thanks for the Memory • and more.

BROADWAY JAZZ STANDARDS Vol. 46 00843042
Ain't Misbehavin' • I've Grown Accustomed to Her Face • Make Someone Happy • Old Devil Moon • Small World • Till There Was You • and more.

CLASSIC JAZZ BALLADS Vol. 47 00843043
Blame It on My Youth • It's Easy to Remember • June in January • Love Letters • A Nightingale Sang in Berkeley Square • When I Fall in Love • and more.

BEBOP CLASSICS Vol. 48 00843044
Be-Bop • Bird Feathers • Blue 'N Boogie • Byrd Like • Cool Blues • Dance of the Indifels • Dexterity • Dizzy Atmosphere • Groovin' High • Tempus Fugit.

MILES DAVIS STANDARDS Vol. 49 00843045
Darn That Dream • I Loves You, Porgy • If I Were a Bell • On Green Dolphin Street • Some Day My Prince Will Come • Yesterdays • and more.

GREAT JAZZ CLASSICS Vol. 50 00843046
Along Came Betty • Birdland • The Jive Samba • Little Sunflower • Nuages • Peri's Scope • Phase Dance • Road Song • Think on Me • Windows.

UP-TEMPO JAZZ Vol. 51 00843047
Cherokee (Indian Love Song) • Chi Chi • 52nd Street Theme • Little Willie Leaps • Move • Pent Up House • Topsy • and more.

STEVIE WONDER Vol. 52 00843048
I Just Called to Say I Love You • Isn't She Lovely • My Cherie Amour • Part Time Lover • Superstition • You Are the Sunshine of My Life • and more.

RHYTHM CHANGES Vol. 53 00843049
Celia • Chasing the Bird • Cotton Tail • Crazeology • Fox Hunt • I Got Rhythm • No Moe • Oleo • Red Cross • Steeplechase.

"MOONLIGHT IN VERMONT" AND OTHER GREAT STANDARDS Vol. 54 00843050
A Child Is Born • Love You Madly • Lover Man (Oh, Where Can You Be?) • Moonlight in Vermont • The Night Has a Thousand Eyes • Small Fry • and more.

BENNY GOLSON Vol. 55 00843052
Along Came Betty • Blues March • Gypsy Jingle-Jangle • I Remember Clifford • Killer Joe • Step Lightly • Whisper Not • and more.

BOOK/CD PACKAGES

ONLY $14.95 EACH!

The Hal Leonard JAZZ PLAY ALONG SERIES is the ultimate learning tool for all jazz musicians. With musician-friendly lead sheets, melody cues and other split track choices on the included CD, this first-of-its-kind package makes learning to play jazz easier and more fun than ever before.

Prices, contents and availability subject to change without notice.

FOR MORE INFORMATION, SEE YOUR LOCAL MUSIC DEALER, OR WRITE TO:

HAL•LEONARD®
CORPORATION

7777 W. BLUEMOUND RD. P.O. BOX 13819
MILWAUKEE, WISCONSIN 53213

Visit Hal Leonard online at
www.halleonard.com

The Best Selling Jazz Book of All Time Is Now Legal!

The Real Books are the most popular jazz books of all time. Since the 1970s, musicians have trusted these volumes to get them through every gig, night after night. The problem is that the books were illegally produced and distributed, without any regard to copyright law, or royalties paid to the composers who created these musical masterpieces.

Hal Leonard is very proud to present the first legitimate and legal editions of these books ever produced. You won't even notice the difference, other than all the notorious errors being fixed: the covers and typeface look the same, the song lists are nearly identical, and the price for our edition is even cheaper than the originals!

Every conscientious musician will appreciate that these books are now produced accurately and ethically, benefitting the songwriters that we owe for some of the greatest tunes of all time!

VOLUME 1

Includes: Autumn Leaves • Black Orpheus • Bluesette • Body and Soul • Don't Get Around Much Anymore • Falling in Love with Love • Footprints • Giant Steps • Have You Met Miss Jones? • Lullaby of Birdland • Misty • Satin Doll • Stella by Starlight • and hundreds more!

00240221	C Edition	$25.00
00240224	Bb Edition	$25.00
00240225	Eb Edition	$25.00
00240226	Bass Clef Edition	$25.00

VOLUME 2

Includes: Avalon • Birdland • Come Rain or Come Shine • Fever • Georgia on My Mind • It Might as Well Be Spring • Moonglow • The Nearness of You • On the Sunny Side of the Street • Route 66 • Sentimental Journey • Smoke Gets in Your Eyes • Tangerine • Yardbird Suite • and more!

| 00240222 | C Edition | $25.00 |

Coming soon:

00240227	Bb Edition	$29.95
00240228	Eb Edition	$29.95
00240229	Bass Clef Edition	$29.95

FOR MORE INFORMATION, SEE YOUR LOCAL MUSIC DEALER, OR WRITE TO:

HAL•LEONARD®
CORPORATION
7777 W. BLUEMOUND RD. P.O. BOX 13819 MILWAUKEE, WI 53213

400 SONGS!

Complete song lists online at www.halleonard.com

Prices and availability subject to change without notice.

1105

Jazz Instruction & Improvisation

Books for All Instruments from Hal Leonard

AN APPROACH TO JAZZ IMPROVISATION

by Dave Pozzi

Musicians Institute Press

Explore the styles of Charlie Parker, Sonny Rollins, Bud Powell and others with this comprehensive guide to jazz improvisation. Covers: scale choices • chord analysis • phrasing • melodies • harmonic progressions • more.

00695135 Book/CD Pack $17.95

BUILDING A JAZZ VOCABULARY

By Mike Steinel

A valuable resource for learning the basics of jazz from Mike Steinel of the University of North Texas. It covers: the basics of jazz • how to build effective solos • a comprehensive practice routine • and a jazz vocabulary of the masters.

00849911 .... $19.95

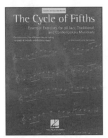

THE CYCLE OF FIFTHS

by Emile and Laura De Cosmo

This essential instruction book provides more than 450 exercises, including hundreds of melodic and rhythmic ideas. The book is designed to help improvisors master the cycle of fifths, one of the primary progressions in music. Guaranteed to refine technique, enhance improvisational fluency, and improve sight-reading!

00311114 .... $14.95

THE DIATONIC CYCLE

by Emile and Laura De Cosmo

Renowned jazz educators Emile and Laura De Cosmo provide more than 300 exercises to help improvisors tackle one of music's most common progressions: the diatonic cycle. This book is guaranteed to refine technique, enhance improvisational fluency, and improve sight-reading!

00311115 .... $16.95

EAR TRAINING

by Keith Wyatt,
Carl Schroeder and Joe Elliott
Musicians Institute Press

Covers: basic pitch matching • singing major and minor scales • identifying intervals • transcribing melodies and rhythm • identifying chords and progressions • seventh chords and the blues • 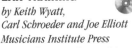 modal interchange, chromaticism, modulation • and more.

00695198 Book/2-CD Pack $19.95

EXERCISES AND ETUDES FOR THE JAZZ INSTRUMENTALIST

by J.J. Johnson

Designed as study material and playable by any instrument, these pieces run the gamut of the jazz experience, featuring common and uncommon time signatures and keys, and styles from ballads to funk. They are progressively graded so that both beginners and professionals will be challenged by the demands of this wonderful music.

00842018 Bass Clef Edition $16.95
00842042 Treble Clef Edition $16.95

JAZZOLOGY

THE ENCYCLOPEDIA OF JAZZ THEORY FOR ALL MUSICIANS

by Robert Rawlins and Nor Eddine Bahha

This comprehensive resource covers a variety of jazz topics, for beginners and pros of any instrument. The book serves as an encyclopedia for reference, a thorough methodology for the student, and a workbook for the classroom.

00311167 .... $17.95

JAZZ THEORY RESOURCES

by Bert Ligon
Houston Publishing, Inc.

This is a jazz theory text in two volumes. **Volume 1 includes:** review of basic theory • rhythm in jazz performance • triadic generalization • diatonic harmonic progressions and analysis • substitutions and turnarounds • and more. **Volume 2 includes:** modes and modal frameworks • quartal harmony • extended tertian structures and triadic superimposition • pentatonic applications • coloring "outside" the lines and beyond • and more.

00030458 Volume 1 .... $39.95
00030459 Volume 2 .... $29.95

JOY OF IMPROV

by Dave Frank and John Amaral

This book/CD course on improvisation for all instruments and all styles will help players develop monster musical skills! **Book One** imparts a solid basis in technique, rhythm, chord theory, ear training and improv concepts. **Book Two** explores more advanced chord voicings, chord arranging techniques and more challenging blues and melodic lines. The CD can be used as a listening and play-along tool.

00220005 Book 1 – Book/CD Pack $24.95
00220006 Book 2 – Book/CD Pack $24.95

THE PATH TO JAZZ IMPROVISATION

by Emile and Laura De Cosmo

This fascinating jazz instruction book offers an innovative, scholarly approach to the art of improvisation. It includes in-depth analysis and lessons about: cycle of fifths • diatonic cycle • overtone series • pentatonic scale • harmonic and melodic minor scale • polytonal order of keys • blues and bebop scales • modes • and more.

00310904 .... $14.95

THE SOURCE

THE DICTIONARY OF CONTEMPORARY AND TRADITIONAL SCALES

by Steve Barta

This book serves as an informative guide for people who are looking for good, solid information regarding scales, chords, and how they work together. It provides right and left hand fingerings for scales, chords, and complete inversions. Includes over 20 different scales, each written in all 12 keys.

00240885 .... $12.95

21 BEBOP EXERCISES

by Steve Rawlins

This book/CD pack is both a warm-up collection and a manual for bebop phrasing. Its tasty and sophisticated exercises will help you develop your proficiency with jazz interpretation. It concentrates on practice in all twelve keys – moving higher by half-step – to help develop dexterity and range. The companion CD includes all of the exercises in 12 keys.

00315341 Book/CD Pack $17.95

THE WOODSHEDDING SOURCE BOOK

by Emile De Cosmo

Rehearsing with this method daily will improve technique, reading ability, rhythmic and harmonic vocabulary, eye/finger coordination, endurance, range, theoretical knowledge, and listening skills – all of which lead to superior improvisational skills.

00842000 C Instruments $19.95

FOR MORE INFORMATION, SEE YOUR LOCAL MUSIC DEALER, OR WRITE TO:

HAL•LEONARD®
CORPORATION

7777 W. BLUEMOUND RD. P.O. BOX 13819 MILWAUKEE, WI 53213

Prices, contents & availability subject to change without notice.

Visit Hal Leonard online at
www.halleonard.com

ARTIST TRANSCRIPTIONS®

Artist Transcriptions are authentic, note-for-note transcriptions of the hottest artists in jazz, pop, and rock today. These outstanding, accurate arrangements are in an easy-to-read format which includes all essential lines. Artist Transcriptions can be used to perform, sequence or reference.

GUITAR & BASS

George Benson
00660113 Guitar Style of $14.95

Pierre Bensusan
00699072 Guitar Book of..................$19.95

Ron Carter
00672331 Acoustic Bass..................$16.95

Stanley Clarke
00672307 The Collection..................$19.95

Al Di Meola
00604041 Cielo E Terra $14.95
00660115 Friday Night in
                San Francisco...............$14.95
00604043 Music, Words, Pictures....$14.95

Tal Farlow
00673245 Jazz Style of $19.95

Bela Fleck and the Flecktones
00672359 Melody/Lyrics/Chords......$18.95

Frank Gambale
00672336 Best of $22.95

Jim Hall
00699389 Jazz Guitar Environments ..$19.95
00699306 Exploring Jazz Guitar $17.95

Allan Holdsworth
00604049 Reaching for the
                Uncommon Chord $14.95

Leo Kottke
00699215 Eight Songs $14.95

Wes Montgomery
00675536 Guitar Transcriptions $17.95

Joe Pass
00672353 The Collection..................$18.95

John Patitucci
00673216 ....$14.95

Django Reinhardt
00027083 Anthology $14.95
00026711 The Genius of $10.95
00026715 A Treasury of Songs $12.95

Johnny Smith
00672374 Guitar Solos $16.95

Mike Stern
00673224 Guitar Book......................$16.95

Mark Whitfield
00672320 Guitar Collection..............$19.95

Gary Willis
00672337 The Collection..................$19.95

SAXOPHONE

Julian "Cannonball" Adderley
00673244 The Collection..................$19.95

Michael Brecker
00673237 ....$19.95
00672429 The Collection..................$19.95

The Brecker Brothers
00672351 And All Their Jazz............$19.95
00672447 Best of $19.95

Benny Carter
00672314 The Collection..................$22.95
00672315 Plays Standards $22.95

James Carter
00672394 The Collection..................$19.95

John Coltrane
00672494 A Love Supreme..............$12.95
00672529 Giant Steps $14.95
00672493 Plays Coltrane Changes...$19.95
00672349 Plays Giant Steps $19.95
00672453 Plays Standards $19.95
00673233 Solos................................$22.95

Paul Desmond
00672328 The Collection..................$19.95
00672454 Standard Time $19.95

Kenny Garrett
00672530 The Collection..................$19.95

Stan Getz
00699375 ....$18.95
00672377 Bossa Novas $19.95
00672375 Standards $17.95

Coleman Hawkins
00672523 The Collection..................$19.95

Joe Henderson
00672330 Best of $22.95
00673252 Selections from Lush Life
                & So Near So Far $19.95

Kenny G
00673239 Best of $19.95
00673229 Breathless........................$19.95
00672462 Classics in the Key of G ..$19.95
00672485 Faith: A Holiday Album....$14.95
00672373 The Moment $19.95
00672516 Paradise $14.95

Joe Lovano
00672326 The Collection..................$19.95

Jackie McLean
00672498 The Collection..................$19.95

James Moody
00672372 The Collection $19.95

Frank Morgan
00672416 The Collection..................$19.95

Sonny Rollins
00672444 The Collection..................$19.95

David Sanborn
00675000 The Collection..................$16.95

Bud Shank
00672528 The Collection..................$19.95

Wayne Shorter
00672498 New Best of $19.95

Lew Tabackin
00672455 The Collection..................$19.95

Stanley Turrentine
00672334 The Collection..................$19.95

Lester Young
00672524 The Collection..................$19.95

PIANO & KEYBOARD

Monty Alexander
00672338 The Collection..................$19.95
00672487 Plays Standards $19.95

Kenny Barron
00672318 The Collection..................$22.95

Count Basie
00672520 The Collection..................$19.95

Warren Bernhardt
00672364 The Collection..................$19.95

Cyrus Chesnut
00672439 The Collection..................$19.95

Billy Childs
00673242 The Collection..................$19.95

Chick Corea
00672300 Paint the World $12.95

Bill Evans
00672537 At Town Hall $16.95
00672365 The Collection..................$19.95
00672425 Piano Interpretations........$19.95
00672510 Trio, Vol. 1: 1959-1961 ..$24.95
00672511 Trio, Vol. 2: 1962-1965 ...$24.95
00672512 Trio, Vol. 3: 1968-1974 ...$24.95
00672513 Trio, Vol. 4: 1979-1980 ....$24.95

Benny Goodman
00672492 The Collection..................$16.95

Benny Green
00672329 The Collection..................$19.95

Vince Guaraldi
00672486 The Collection..................$19.95

Herbie Hancock
00672419 The Collection..................$19.95

Gene Harris
00672446 The Collection..................$19.95

Hampton Hawes
00672438 The Collection..................$19.95

Ahmad Jamal
00672322 The Collection..................$22.95

CLARINET

Buddy De Franco
00672423 The Collection..................$19.95

FLUTE

Eric Dolphy
00672379 The Collection..................$19.95

James Moody
00672372 The Collection $19.95

James Newton
00660108 Improvising Flute $14.95

Lew Tabackin
00672455 The Collection..................$19.95

TROMBONE

J.J. Johnson
00672332 The Collection..................$19.95

Brad Mehldau
00672476 The Collection..................$19.95

Thelonious Monk
00672388 Best of $19.95
00672389 The Collection..................$19.95
00672390 Jazz Standards, Vol. 1 ....$19.95
00672391 Jazz Standards, Vol. 2 ....$19.95
00672392 Intermediate Piano Solos..$14.95

Jelly Roll Morton
00672433 The Piano Rolls.................$12.95

Oscar Peterson
00672531 Plays Duke Ellington $19.95
00672534 Very Best of $19.95

Michael Petrucciani
00673226 ....$17.95

Bud Powell
00672371 Classics $19.95
00672376 The Collection..................$19.95

André Previn
00672437 The Collection..................$19.95

Gonzalo Rubalcaba
00672507 The Collection $19.95

Horace Silver
00672303 The Collection..................$19.95

Art Tatum
00672316 The Collection..................$22.95
00672355 Solo Book $19.95

Billy Taylor
00672357 The Collection..................$24.95

McCoy Tyner
00673215 ....$16.95

Cedar Walton
00672321 The Collection..................$19.95

Kenny Werner
00672519 The Collection..................$19.95

Teddy Wilson
00672434 The Collection..................$19.95

TRUMPET

Louis Armstrong
00672480 The Collection..................$14.95
00672481 Plays Standards $14.95

Chet Baker
00672435 The Collection..................$19.95

Randy Brecker
00673234 ....$17.95

The Brecker Brothers
00672351 And All Their Jazz............$19.95
00672447 Best of $19.95

Miles Davis
00672448 Originals, Vol. 1 ....$19.95
00672451 Originals, Vol. 2 ....$19.95
00672450 Standards, Vol. 1 ....$19.95
00672449 Standards, Vol. 2 ....$19.95

Dizzy Gillespie
00672479 The Collection..................$19.95

Freddie Hubbard
00673214 ....$14.95

Tom Harrell
00672382 Jazz Trumpet Solos $19.95

Chuck Mangione
00672506 The Collection..................$19.95

FOR MORE INFORMATION, SEE YOUR LOCAL MUSIC DEALER,
OR WRITE TO:

HAL•LEONARD® CORPORATION

7777 W. BLUEMOUND RD. P.O. BOX 13819 MILWAUKEE, WI 53213

**Visit our web site for a complete listing
of our titles with songlists at
www.halleonard.com**

Prices and availability subject to change without notice.

0105